STATUE OF LIBERTY

Jennifer Hurtig and Heather Kissock

www.av2books.com

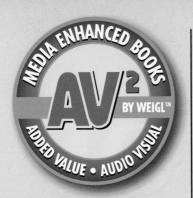

AV² provides enriched content that supplements and complements this book. Weigl's AV² books strive to create inspired learning and engage young minds in a total learning experience.

Your AV² Media Enhanced books come alive with...

Audio
Listen to sections of the book read aloud.

Key Words
Study vocabulary, and complete a matching word activity.

Video
Watch informative video clips.

Quizzes
Test your knowledge.

Embedded Weblinks
Gain additional information for research.

Slide Show
View images and captions, and prepare a presentation.

Try This!
Complete activities and hands-on experiments.

... and much, much more!

Go to **www.av2books.com**, and enter this book's unique code.

BOOK CODE

S632421

AV² by Weigl brings you media enhanced books that support active learning.

Published by AV² by Weigl
350 5th Avenue, 59th Floor
New York, NY 10118
Websites: www.av2books.com www.weigl.com

Library of Congress Cataloging-in-Publication Data

Hurtig, Jennifer.
The Statue of Liberty / Jennifer Hurtig and Heather Kissock.
    pages cm. -- (Virtual field trip)
Includes bibliographical references and index.
ISBN 978-1-4896-1966-2 (hard cover : alk. paper) -- ISBN 978-1-4896-1967-9 (soft cover : alk. paper) --
ISBN 978-1-4896-1968-6 (single use ebook) -- ISBN 978-1-4896-1969-3 (multi use ebook)
1. Statue of Liberty (New York, N.Y.)--Juvenile literature. 2. New York (N.Y.)--Buildings, structures, etc.--Juvenile literature. I. Kissock, Heather. II. Title.
 F128.64.L6H872 2014
 974.7'1--dc23

                          2014009435

Printed in the United States of America in North Mankato, Minnesota
1 2 3 4 5 6 7 8 9 0 18 17 16 15 14

052014
WEP310514

Editor: Heather Kissock
Design: Terry Paulhus

Every reasonable effort has been made to trace ownership and to obtain permission to reprint copyright material. The publishers would be pleased to have any errors or omissions brought to their attention so that they may be corrected in subsequent printings.

Weigl acknowledges Getty Images and Alamy as its primary image suppliers for this title.

Contents

What Is the Statue of Liberty?

The Statue of Liberty is one of the planet's best-known monuments. Also known as Liberty Enlightening the World, it stands as a symbol of the United States of America. It marks the principles of **democracy** and freedom on which that country is based. The statue represents liberty and escape from **oppression**.

The Statue of Liberty was given to the United States by France in 1886. It was a gift for the centennial of America's Declaration of Independence. It also celebrated the friendship between the two nations. Both France and the United States share similar histories. They waged wars in the 1700s to become **republics** that were free from the rule of a **monarch**.

France was a key ally during the American Revolution. It supplied the United States with weapons, soldiers, and funds. France shared in the American victory and sought to copy the United States. Presenting the United States with a gift to mark its centennial seemed an appropriate way to show France's respect and admiration. It also was seen as a way of promoting France's current government. When the idea for this gift was created, many people in France wanted a return to the rule of a monarch. Politicians believed that giving this large gift to a fellow republic would encourage the people of France to maintain their current system of government.

The Statue of Liberty features a woman lifting a torch in her right hand. She is stepping out of the shackles that bind her. These elements help to show how the statue represents freedom.

Snapshot of New York State

New York State is located in the northeastern part of the United States. It shares its southern border with New Jersey and Pennsylvania and its northern border with the Canadian provinces of Ontario and Quebec. Connecticut, Massachusetts, and Vermont lie to its east.

INTRODUCING NEW YORK

CAPITAL CITY: Albany

FLAG:

MOTTO: *Excelsior* (Ever Upward)

NICKNAME: The Empire State

POPULATION: 19,465,197 (2011)

ADMITTED TO THE UNION: July 26, 1788

CLIMATE: Warm and humid summers with cold winters

SUMMER TEMPERATURE: Average of 82 Fahrenheit (28° Celsius)

WINTER TEMPERATURE: Average of –7° F (–22° C)

TIME ZONE: Eastern Standard Time (EST)

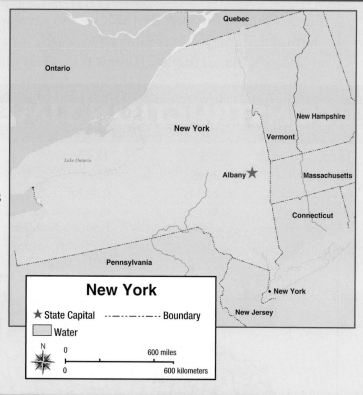

New York Symbols

New York has several official symbols. Some symbols represent the features that distinguish the area from other parts of the United States. Others indicate the unique place New York has in the history of the country.

OFFICIAL FLOWER
Rose

OFFICIAL BIRD
Eastern Bluebird

OFFICIAL TREE
Sugar Maple

A Step Back in Time

The idea to build a statue was first proposed in 1865 at a dinner party attended by French sculptor, Frédéric Auguste Bartholdi. During dinner, conversation turned to the United States and its success in building a democratic nation after years of British rule. Even though the centennial was 11 years away, the people at the dinner party felt that France should give a gift to the United States.

Bartholdi liked the idea. By 1871, he had developed a concept for the statue. Bartholdi journeyed to New York to search for a site to place it. When he arrived at Bedloe's Island, Bartholdi knew that it was the perfect site for his statue.

CONSTRUCTION TIMELINE

1865
The plan to build a statue is hatched at a dinner party in France.

1875
Bartholdi's model is approved. Construction starts.

1877
The U.S. government designates Bedloe's Island as the future home of the statue.

1883
Construction begins on the pedestal, or base, of the statue.

1884
The statue is completed in France.

As a joint effort between the two countries, it was agreed that the pedestal would be built in the United States and the statue in France.

The United States agreed with Bartholdi's plans. Upon returning to France, he set to work on a model of the statue. After the model was approved in 1875, Bartholdi hired Gustave Eiffel to design the framework for the statue. Eiffel was well-known for building metal structures, such as the Eiffel Tower in Paris, France.

One of Bartholdi's models for the Statue of Liberty now stands in Paris's Jardin du Luxembourg.

1885
The statue is shipped in pieces to the United States.

1886
The pedestal is completed in April. On October 28, the completed Statue of Liberty is dedicated.

1982
Plans for restoring the Statue of Liberty are put into place.

1984
The restoration begins. The statue is designated as a **UNESCO World Heritage Site**.

July 5, 1986
The restoration of the Statue of Liberty is complete.

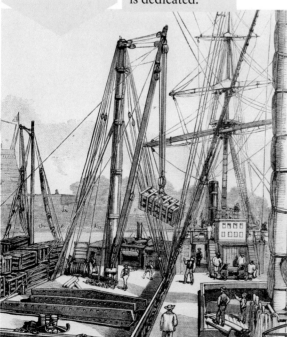
The statue was so large that it had to be split into 350 pieces and packed in 214 crates for shipping. During its voyage, the ship almost sank because of the weight.

The restoration project was undertaken to celebrate the Statue of Liberty's centennial.

The Statue of Liberty's Location

Located in the New York harbor, the Statue of Liberty was one of the first **landmarks** immigrants to the United States saw when they arrived by ship. To many of these people, the statue symbolized what they hoped to find in America—freedom and acceptance. The sight of the Statue of Liberty gave them hope for a fresh start and a new future.

Once called Bedloe's Island, the island on which the Statue of Liberty stands was renamed Liberty Island in 1956. The statue itself stands on the site of a former fort. Fort Wood was built to protect New York City from invasion during the War of 1812. The statue was built within the walls of the fort. The fort was later torn down.

People arrive on the island via two ferry routes. One route originates in New York City, while the other starts in New Jersey. The statue is actually closer to New Jersey than the city of New York. In fact, the Statue of Liberty is located in New Jersey waters.

Liberty Island has a long history with the United States. As early as 994 AD, American Indians fished and hunted on the island.

The Statue of Liberty Today

The Statue of Liberty and the island on which it sits are now part of the National Park Service. Park rangers offer daily tours and talks that provide background information regarding the statue's construction and **symbolism**. Approximately 4 million people visit the Statue of Liberty every year to experience the monument and understand its significance in the country's history.

Face The face of the Statue of liberty is more than 8 feet (2.4 m) tall.

8 feet (2.4 m)

35 feet (10.7 m)

151.1 feet (46.05 m)

Waist Lady Liberty's waist is 35 feet (10.7 m) around.

Height The total height of the Statue of Liberty from the ground to the torch is 305.1 feet (92.99 m). The statue measures 151.1 feet (46.05 m) from the top of the base to the top of the torch.

305.1 feet (92.99 m)

Weight The weight of the Statue of Liberty is 450,000 pounds (204,117 kilograms). The metal used in the statue weighs a total of 312,000 pounds (141,521 kg). The concrete **foundation** of the statue weighs 54 million pounds (24,493,988 kg).

Statue of Liberty Features

From its tip to its base, Bartholdi put much thought into the design of the Statue of Liberty. Almost every detail of the statue has symbolic meaning, leading to the idea of liberty enlightening the world.

Head At the top of the statue, a crown rests upon the woman's head. The crown has seven spikes. These spikes represent the seven seas and seven continents of the world. They represent the idea that people all over the world should have the right to freedom. The crown has 25 windows. Rays of sunlight reflect upward from the windows, symbolizing the way a person seems to glow when he or she has been enlightened.

Bartholdi's mother, Charlotte, is often believed to have been the model for the Statue of Liberty's face.

The date on the tablet is written in Roman numerals. The tablet itself measures 23 feet 7 inches (7.2 m) tall and 13 feet 7 inches (4.2 m) wide.

Tablet Lady Liberty carries a tablet in her left hand. The tablet represents the law and principles on which the United States is founded. The date of America's independence, July 4, 1776, is written on the tablet. The tablet is placed near Lady Liberty's heart. This may be to remind people of the importance of Independence Day.

Torch The statue features a woman lifting a torch in her right hand. The torch represents enlightenment. Its light shows people the path to freedom.

The torch is not open to the public. However, in 2011, five webcams were placed inside the torch to allow people to experience the view from this part of the statue.

Base Even the base of the statue is symbolic. It is made up of 13 layers of granite. These layers represent the 13 founding colonies of the United States. A poem about freedom is inscribed on a plaque that was placed on the inner wall of the pedestal. Emma Lazarus wrote the poem to help raise funds for the pedestal. Today, the plaque is part of an exhibit inside the pedestal.

The pedestal, or base, is about half the size of the entire monument.

A stola is the female version of a toga, which the men of Ancient Rome wore.

Clothing The woman wears an ancient Roman style of clothing consisting of a stola, or robe, and cloak. The clothing is similar to that worn by the Roman goddess "Libertas." This goddess was worshiped by people who had been freed from slavery.

VIRTUAL TOUR

From 1886 to 1902, the Statue of Liberty was used as a lighthouse.

Touring the Statue of Liberty

Liberty Island is a showcase for the Statue of Liberty. The National Park Service has provided a variety of learning opportunities for visitors to the site. These allow visitors to explore and experience the statue and its history in several ways.

Visitors Information Center One of the first places people visit when they arrive on Liberty Island is the Visitors Information Center. Here, they can arrange a guided tour with a park ranger. They can also view a video introduction to the statue and island. The center has a selection of brochures that provide information on the Statue of Liberty and the island itself. Self-guided audio tours are available for visitors who want to tour the site on their own.

Ferries deliver people to the island's landing dock. From there, it is short walk to the statue.

The Statue of Liberty's original torch was removed during the statue's restoration. It is now on display at the entrance to museum.

Liberty Island Museum The Liberty Island Museum tells the story of the Statue of Liberty's construction. Displays and artifacts detail the challenges the builders faced and the decisions that had to be made to make the statue a reality. The museum also explores the statue's meaning and how this meaning has changed over time to reflect shifting priorities and trends in American culture.

Crown Level Visitors wanting the ultimate Statue of Liberty experience can climb the 377 steps to the statue's crown. Here, they can gaze out of the crown's windows for a view of New York City, New Jersey, and the surrounding waters. The stairs have been designed in a double spiral, allowing for easy access up and down. Still, people must be in good shape to make the trek. There are no elevators in this part of the statue.

No more than 15 people are allowed to enter the crown at a time due its limited space.

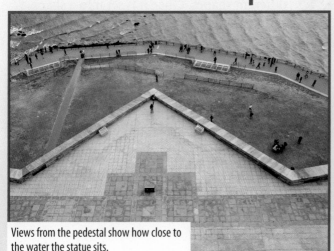

Views from the pedestal show how close to the water the statue sits.

Pedestal Level The pedestal rises 154 feet (46.9 m) from the base and features several observation levels. Visitors to this part of the statue have the option of climbing stairs or taking an elevator to each level. There are 215 steps from the lobby to the top of the pedestal.

Fort Wood Level The Statue of Liberty sits in the middle of an 11-pointed star. This star once formed the walls of Fort Wood. The walls are made of stone and are approximately 20 feet (6.1 m) thick at their base. The fort's main door now serves as the entrance to the statue. As visitors walk down the corridor to the elevators and stairways, they pass by several plaques that offer information on the statue.

People can walk on the fort's former promenade. This platform that surrounds the statue was once where the fort's guns were positioned.

Big Ideas behind the Statue of Liberty

While planning the construction of the Statue of Liberty, Bartholdi had to think about the outdoor environment in which it would be sitting. The statue would face many types of weather, ranging from high winds to rain to snow. The salty **humidity** of the ocean air also could damage the statue. Bartholdi had to use durable materials that would withstand the environment.

People climbing to and from the crown can see the iron framework that Gustave Eiffel designed for the statue.

The Properties of Iron

Iron is a versatile and strong material. With the use of heat, it easily can be molded into different shapes. Once it is set into a shape, iron stays firmly in position. It carries the weight of the other materials involved in the structure. This was very helpful when creating the framework inside the Statue of Liberty. The inner framework of the statue is made up of four iron posts that run from the bottom to the top of the statue. The posts form a pylon at the top to bear the weight of the statue. Smaller beams come from the central tower of iron. These beams support the statue's shell.

The Properties of Copper

The shell, or outside, of the statue is made up of copper sheets that have been fastened to the frame. One of the main advantages of using copper on the outside of the statue is that it does not corrode, or rust, easily. This means that it can face all kinds of weather, including wind, rain, snow, and sunlight, without being degraded. Copper is easily molded. This allows workers to shape the sheets into the statue's parts.

While copper is a reddish-orange color, the Statue of Liberty is green. Humidity, wind, and other forms of weather have interacted with the copper, causing a coating, or patina, to appear. This patina actually protects the copper from corrosion.

Science at Work at the Statue of Liberty

Bartholdi made several scale models of the statue before construction began. The final, quarter-scale model was cut into 300 pieces. Bartholdi and his workers measured each piece. They then multiplied the measurements by four to reach the final size of the statue. This made sure that the full-size statue would look just like the model. To build the final statue, Bartholdi used many tools.

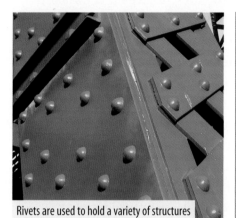

Rivets are used to hold a variety of structures together, from statues to bridges.

Rivets

To connect the sheets of copper that make up the outer layer of the statue, workers used metal rivets. Rivets look like stubby nails. They have a thick, blunt shaft, with a round head at one end. Rivets are very good at resisting a force called shear. Shear is the force that pulls **perpendicular** to the shaft of the rivet. In the Statue of Liberty, shear occurs when one heavy copper sheet pulls down on the sheet above it. The builders of the statue used many rivets to make sure that each rivet would have less shear to deal with on its own. This meant that each single rivet would be less likely to break.

Mallets

To create the outer shell of the statue, workers pounded thin sheets of copper onto each piece. They did this using tools called mallets. Mallet heads can be made out of many different materials. Some mallets are made from materials such as wood and rubber. They are used for working with soft metals, such as copper, because they do not leave dents or marks. Mallets are designed to swing faster and hit harder than human arms. This is a property of tools is called mechanical advantage. Mechanical advantage tools can accomplish more work with the same effort.

Mallets are used in various forms of construction, from sculpting to laying bricks.

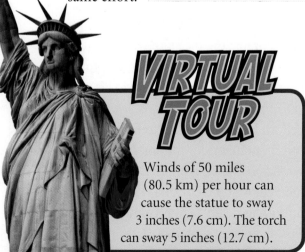

VIRTUAL TOUR

Winds of 50 miles (80.5 km) per hour can cause the statue to sway 3 inches (7.6 cm). The torch can sway 5 inches (12.7 cm).

The Statue of Liberty's Builders

Frédéric Bartholdi planned all aspects of the Statue of Liberty before it was built. He picked a location, took measurements of the location, determined the materials the statue would be made of, and decided exactly how the statue would be built. To complete the construction of the Statue of Liberty, Bartholdi needed the help of many trade specialists, including metalworkers and laborers.

Bartholdi discovered his love of large structures after a visit to see the pyramids of Egypt.

Frédéric Auguste Bartholdi

Sculptor

Frédéric Auguste Bartholdi was born on August 2, 1834, in Colmar, a town in the French province of Alsace. It was in Alsace that he first began training to be an **architect**. Bartholdi later moved to Paris to study painting and sculpture. Over time, he gained a reputation for creating large-scale sculptures. After completing the Statue of Liberty, he was contracted to create more sculptures. In France, his work can be found in his hometown of Colmar, as well as in Paris, Lyon, and Belfort. He also designed fountains, statues, and monuments for the cities of Boston, New York, and Washington, DC. Bartholdi died of tuberculosis on October 4, 1904, in Paris. At the time of his death, he was considered one of the world's greatest sculptors.

Gustave Eiffel Engineer

Alexandre-Gustave Eiffel was born in 1832 in Dijon, France. As a child, he showed an interest in science. He later studied chemistry and graduated from the Ecole Centrale des Arts and Manufactures, one of Europe's top engineering schools. Upon graduation, Eiffel took a job with an engineering firm. By the age of 25, he was working on bridges and other major projects. Eventually, he formed his own company, specializing in railway bridges and viaducts. Following the construction of the Statue of Liberty, Eiffel began work on what would become his best-known project, the Eiffel Tower, in Paris. The tower was completed in 1889.

Eiffel was the second person hired to design the Statue of Liberty's internal framework. He replaced Eugene Viollet-le-Duc, who died part of the way through the project.

Sculptors

Sculptors are artists who design and build three-dimensional works of art. Sculpture can be created from many types of materials, such as stone, clay, and metal. Some sculptors carve sculptures from these materials. Others use molds to create shapes. Sculptors can use a variety of tools to create art. They may use their hands to mold materials into shape. Knives and **chisels** help chip pieces of rock. Mallets are used to pound softer materials. Sometimes, the materials are placed in a kiln. The heat sets the sculpture in a certain form.

Sculptors usually specialize in certain types of materials. Some may prefer to work with copper, while others work with clay.

Metalworkers

Metalworkers were very important in the construction of the Statue of Liberty. They were responsible for putting all of the pieces in place. Metalworkers work with a set of blueprints to show them how the pieces of the structure fit together. They install the pieces by bolting or riveting them into place. Sometimes, metalworkers may weld pieces together. This involves applying heat to the metal to **fuse** the pieces together. Metalworkers must have knowledge of different metals. They should also know the most effective methods and tools for working with metals.

Metalworkers often use heat to shape things out of metal.

Construction laborers are skilled in a number of tasks. This allows them to help in a variety of areas on the job site.

Laborers

Laborers play a key role at any construction site. They get the materials into the hands of the people who need them. They do this by carrying the materials on their shoulders, carting them in wheelbarrows, and loading them onto trucks. Laborers help keep job sites clean. They know how to use tools, such as saws and hammers, and can operate a variety of construction equipment.

Similar Structures around the World

Statues have been built and displayed all around the world. Each was built with its own purpose in mind. Some commemorate war heroes or are tributes to beauty. Others honor religious figures. All are meant to inspire those who view them.

Christ the Redeemer

BUILT: 1931
LOCATION: Corcovado Mountain, Rio de Janeiro, Brazil
DESIGN: Heitor da Silva Costa and Paul Landowski
DESCRIPTION: This statue of Jesus Christ with outstretched arms is one of the **New Seven Wonders of the World**. The exterior is made of soapstone, and the inside is made of concrete. The statue stands as a symbol of **Christianity**.

The Venus de Milo was sculpted from two blocks of marble. The individual pieces of the sculpture were attached to each other using pegs.

The Christ the Redeemer statue stands 98 feet (30 m) tall. Its arms extend almost the same distance, measuring 92 feet (28 m) across.

Venus de Milo

BUILT: Around 190–100 BC
LOCATION: The Louvre in Paris, France
DESIGN: Alexandros of Antioch
DESCRIPTION: This marble statue is believed to represent Aphrodite, the Greek goddess of romantic love. It was found buried in ancient city ruins on the Aegean island of Milos. The statue was found in two pieces. These pieces were put together when the statue reached the Louvre. The arms were too damaged to be reattached.

Great Sphinx of Giza

BUILT: Around 2500 BC
LOCATION: Giza Plateau, Egypt
DESIGN: King Khafre
DESCRIPTION: The Great Sphinx is believed to have been built to guard King Khafre's temple. Made out of limestone, the Sphinx is a statue of a creature that is half-lion and half-human, with eagle wings. It remains a mystery as to what this statue represents.

The Leshan Buddha is made almost entirely of stone. Only its ears are made of another material. They are made of wood and clay.

The Sphinx is one of the world's largest statues made from a single stone. It stands higher than a six-story building.

Leshan Buddha

BUILT: Started in 713 AD
LOCATION: near Leshan, China
DESIGN: Haitong
DESCRIPTION: The tallest stone Buddha in the world is also one of the world's oldest sculptures. It was carved out of the side of a cliff and has three rivers flowing at its feet. A Chinese monk named Haitong planned the building of this Buddha to calm the rough waters that made it difficult for boats to sail down the river.

Issues Facing the Statue of Liberty

The environment can have a large effect on a statue. The Statue of Liberty is in an area that faces many types of weather and pollution. In the early 1980s, the statue was inspected to assess the damage that its environment had caused. The inspectors decided that the statue had to be restored.

WHAT WAS THE ISSUE?

The humid air of the harbor had caused rust stains to appear on the statue's exterior skin.	**Galvanic corrosion** caused the iron framework to swell and distort.

EFFECTS

The rust was causing corrosion on the interior iron frame.	The movement pulled many of the rivets out from the copper pieces that were holding them in place.

ACTION TAKEN

Stainless steel was used to replace some of the iron bars, and steps were taken to reduce contact between the metals that made up the interior frame and the copper skin.	Workers had to replace more than 30,000 copper within the statue.

Testing Corrosion

Copper and iron were used to build the Statue of Liberty because they are very durable metals. Try this experiment to see which metal corrodes the fastest. You will need to observe the metals over a 10-day period and make notes every day.

Materials
- Two pieces silver wire
- Two pieces copper wire
- Two pieces iron wire
- Six clear drinking glasses
- Six pencils
- Salt
- Distilled water
- A sheet of paper

Instructions
1. Cut the paper to make six labels. Mark each of the labels as follows: a) water and silver; b) salt water and silver; c) water and copper; d) salt water and copper; e) water and steel; f) salt water and steel.

2. Set the glasses in a row on a counter, and place one label in front of each glass.

3. Fill three of the glasses with distilled water, and place with the appropriate label.

4. Mix 3 cups of water with 2 tablespoons of salt until the salt is dissolved.

5. Fill the remaining three cups with the salt water.

6. Wrap one end of each piece of wire around a pencil, leaving enough wire to touch the bottom of the glass.

7. Balance the pencil on the top of each marked glass, and hang the wire into the water and salt water.

8. Check on the wires every day for the next 10 days. Look for changes such as rust. Observe and compare if the wire corroded more in the distilled water or salt water. Watch for where the metal rusts—if it is only on one part of the wire or all over.

Statue of Liberty Quiz

Q What does the Statue of Liberty symbolize?

A The statue symbolizes liberty and the escape from oppression.

Q Who drew the plans for the Statue of Liberty?

A Frédéric Auguste Bartholdi

Q Which two metals make up most of the statue?

A Copper and iron

Q Why did the Statue of Liberty need to be restored in 1984?

A The statue needed to be restored due to damage caused by corrosion.

Key Words

architect: a person who designs buildings

chisels: hand tools consisting of a flat steel blade with a handle

Christianity: a religion that believes in and follows the teachings of Jesus Christ

democracy: a form of government in which the public directs policy through its representatives

foundation: the part of a building that helps support its weight

fuse: unite by melting

galvanic corrosion: when two types of metal come into contact near electrical activity

humidity: the amount of moisture in the air

landmarks: certain objects on Earth that can be used to mark a piece of land

monarch: a king or queen

New Seven Wonders of the World: the seven structures considered by scholars to be the most wondrous of the modern world

oppression: a feeling of being weighed down within a person's mind or body

perpendicular: at right angles

republics: states in which the supreme power is held by the people and not by a king or queen

symbolism: the practice of using one thing to represent something else

UNESCO World Heritage Site: a site designated by the United Nations to be of great cultural worth to the world and in need of protection

Index

Log on to www.av2books.com

AV² by Weigl brings you media enhanced books that support active learning. Go to www.av2books.com, and enter the special code found on page 2 of this book. You will gain access to enriched and enhanced content that supplements and complements this book. Content includes video, audio, weblinks, quizzes, a slide show, and activities.

AV² Online Navigation

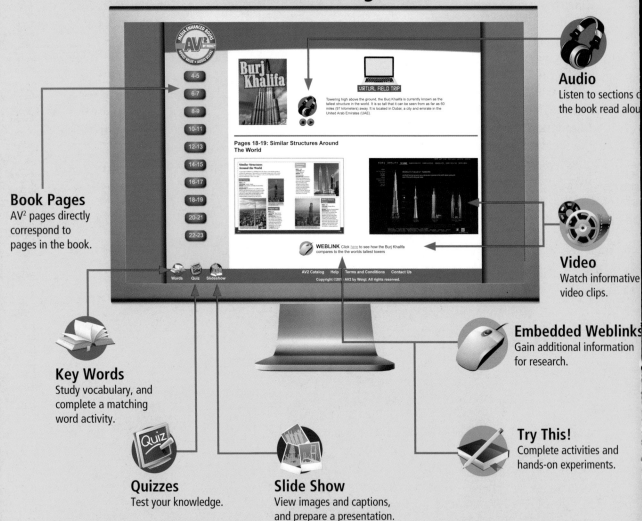

Book Pages
AV² pages directly correspond to pages in the book.

Audio
Listen to sections of the book read aloud

Video
Watch informative video clips.

Key Words
Study vocabulary, and complete a matching word activity.

Embedded Weblinks
Gain additional information for research.

Quizzes
Test your knowledge.

Slide Show
View images and captions, and prepare a presentation.

Try This!
Complete activities and hands-on experiments.

AV² was built to bridge the gap between print and digital. We encourage you to tell us what you like and what you want to see in the future.

Sign up to be an AV² Ambassador at www.av2books.com/ambassador.